## A New True Book

# YOSEMITE

# NATIONAL PARK

**By David Petersen**

CHILDRENS PRESS®

CHICAGO

Nevada Fall and Liberty Cap
are in Yosemite National Park.

PHOTO CREDITS

The Bettmann Archive—11

© John Elk III—9, 12, 13, 27, 28

© Virginia R. Grimes—19, 25

H. Armstrong Roberts—© Joura, Cover; © G. L. French, 2, 18 (left), 40; © D. Muench, 4; © Leonard Lee Rue III, 29

Kirkendall/Spring—6, 15 (left)

North Wind Picture Archives—10 (left)

Photograph Courtesy of the National Park Service—© Julius Boysen, 8 (Neg. No. RL-14, 120)

PhotoEdit—© David Young-Wolff, 17, 30 (right), 38, 39, 42 (right); © Jose Carrillo, 45

© Carl Purcell—26

Root Resources—© James Blank, 23; © Anthony Mercieca, 32; © Alan G. Nelson, 36 (left); © Jana R. Jirak, 44

Tom Stack & Associates—© John Gerlach, 16; © Brian Parker, 35 (left)

SuperStock International, Inc.—© Mick Roessler, 14; © Steve Vidler, 18 (right); © Kurt Scholz, 20, © Michael Frye, 33 (left)

TSW-CLICK/Chicago—© L.L.T. Rhodes, 42 (left)

Valan—© Phillip Norton, 15 (right); © Bob Gurr, 30 (left); © Esther Schmidt, 33 (right); © Dennis W. Schmidt, 34 (left); © Robert C. Simpson, 34 (right); © Tom W. Parkin, 35 (right); © Wayne Lankinen, 36 (right); © Jeff Foott, 37

Horizon Graphics map—4 (bottom)

Cover—El Capitan & Bridalveil Fall, Yosemite National Park

Horizon Graphics map—4 (top)

Cover—El Capitan & Bridalveil Fall, Yosemite National Park

Library of Congress Cataloging-in-Publication Data

Petersen, David.
    Yosemite National Park / by David Petersen.
        p.    cm. — (A New true book)
    Includes index.
    Summary: Describes the mountains, waterfalls, glaciers, Giant Sequoia trees, wildlife, and other sights of interest in California's Yosemite National Park.
    ISBN 0-516-01335-1
    1.   Natural history—California—Yosemite National Park—Juvenile literature.   2.   Yosemite National Park (Calif.)—Juvenile literature.   [1.   Yosemite National Park (Calif.)   2.   National parks and reserves.]   I.  Title.
QH105.C2P48   1993
508.794'47—dc20

Project Editor: Fran Dyra
Design: Margrit Fiddle

# TABLE OF CONTENTS

Cathedral Rocks tower above the valley at Yosemite.

# A PLACE OF GIANTS

In eastern California, there is a place of giants. It is Yosemite National Park.

The first people ever to see Yosemite country were the Native Americans who came there more than 2,000 years ago. Even today, the sheer size of Yosemite's natural wonders amazes visitors.

Yosemite's mountains, the Sierra Nevada, are gigantic.

Huge Yosemite Valley is walled in by towering granite cliffs.

A species of tree that grows in Yosemite, the giant sequoia, can be hundreds of feet tall.

Until recently, giant grizzly bears made Yosemite country their home. Today, Yosemite's grizzlies are gone. But all the other giants are still there, waiting for you to visit.

Opposite page: The Lost Arrow rock formation stands 3,000 feet above the floor of Yosemite Valley.

A Mono Lake
Paiute mother
and child.

# HUMAN HISTORY

For hundreds of years, the Southern Miwok and Mono Lake Paiutes had Yosemite all to themselves. They hunted, fished, and gathered wild plants for food and medicines.

A Miwok village roundhouse

The Native Americans
probably could have lived
forever in balance with
nature in Yosemite. But in
the middle 1800s, white
settlers discovered
Yosemite country.

They forced the Native
Americans out. They built

9

These drawings show some of the first white settlers coming into Yosemite Valley (left) and the first log cabin that they built.

houses and roads. They cut down the forests for timber. They tunneled into the mountains for minerals. And they killed much of the wildlife.

Had this destruction continued, there would be little of Yosemite's wild beauty left today.

# A PARK IS BORN

John Muir

Fortunately, some people thought Yosemite should be preserved for all time. John Muir, a writer and naturalist, was one of the friends of Yosemite. Through the efforts of Muir and others, Yosemite became a national park in 1890.

Tuolumne Meadows at an elevation of 8600 feet
lies within the Sierra Nevada.

Yosemite National Park–
the place of giants–is huge.
It is 748,542 acres of
mountains, forests, meadows,
streams, and lakes. That's
more than 1,169 square
miles of wild beauty!

And more than 94 percent of the park—706,348 acres—is preserved as wilderness. No roads, buildings, or cars are allowed in this wilderness. No one lives there. This helps keep the park healthy and natural.

Fall foliage at Merced River

Visitors can ride horses to see the park's wilderness areas.

# SEEING YOSEMITE

Yosemite has changed a lot since the time when American Indians were the only humans there. Today, the park is one of America's most popular vacation spots.

Each year, millions of people visit Yosemite. They camp, hike, fish, swim, canoe, ride horses and bicycles, explore, take pictures, ski (in winter), and tour the park's visitor centers and museums.

A hiker (left) checks a map of the park's trails. These Japanese tourists (right) are some of the many people who travel thousands of miles to visit Yosemite.

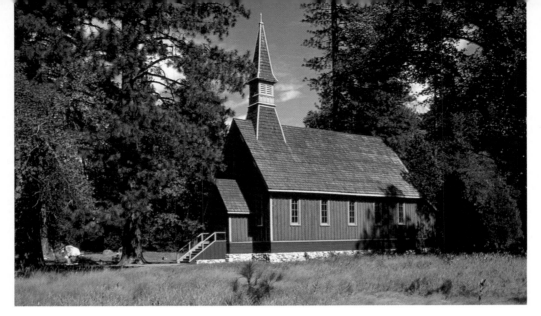

Yosemite Valley Chapel

# YOSEMITE VALLEY

The busiest part of the park is Yosemite Valley. In some places, the valley resembles a town. There are hotels, stores, restaurants, a church, offices, a gas station,

A shuttle bus at Yosemite

parking lots—even a jail
and a dentist's office.

In summer, Yosemite
Valley even has traffic
jams. But you don't need
a car to get around there.
The valley has a free
shuttle-bus service to take
visitors from place to place.

17

Half Dome (left) and El Capitan (right) are two of Yosemite's most famous rock features.

And much of Yosemite Valley remains quiet and unspoiled. There are forests, meadows, a lake, streams, campgrounds, and wild animals.

People with proper training and equipment can go climbing on

Rock climbers on El Capitan

Yosemite's high cliffs. Two
of the most popular cliffs,
or "faces," for rock climbers
are Half Dome and El Capitan.
Visitors in the valley can see
the tiny figures of climbers
inching their way up these
vertical rock faces.

# WATERFALLS

Thirteen waterfalls tumble over cliffs into Yosemite Valley. Like everything else about Yosemite, its waterfalls are giants. In fact, Yosemite has two of the ten highest waterfalls in the world.

The highest of the park's falls is Yosemite Falls. Its roaring waters race down three stair-step falls—Upper, Middle, and Lower—for a

Opposite page: Yosemite Falls

total drop of 2,425 feet. That makes it the highest waterfall in North America—and the fifth-highest in the world.

A big waterfall is so powerful that it makes the ground tremble. The rumble of Yosemite's giant waterfalls can be heard from miles away. Getting too close to a big waterfall is dangerous.

Bridalveil Fall drops 620 feet to the valley below.

# GLACIERS

Yosemite's waterfalls—like its valleys, cliffs, and lakes—were shaped by huge sheets of ice called glaciers. A glacier is made of thousands of tons of ice formed when heavy layers of snow are pressed together.

Yosemite's glaciers were formed many thousands of years ago, when the climate was much colder.

Gradually, these ice fields slid down the mountains and through Yosemite Valley. Their hard, sharp edges carved and shaped the land as they crept along.

These big rocks, called erratics, were left behind by melting glaciers.

Much later, the climate grew warmer again and the glaciers melted. When they had gone, Yosemite looked much as it does today.

The work of ancient ice in Yosemite can be seen

View of Yosemite Valley from Glacier Point

from Glacier Point. It is the most beautiful view of Yosemite you can reach without a long walk. Exhibits at Glacier Point explain how the glaciers shaped Yosemite.

Giant sequoias tower over the Galen Clark cabin in the Mariposa Grove.

# GIANT SEQUOIAS

Sequoias are the largest living things in the world. Some giant sequoia trees are close to 3,000 years old, 300 feet tall, and 35 feet in diameter.

To see the best of Yosemite's giant sequoias, visit the Mariposa Grove. The biggest sequoia there is the Grizzly Giant. It is 200 feet tall and 31 feet in diameter.

The Grizzly Giant sequoia is more than 2,700 years old.

# WILDLIFE

Grizzlies, like this mother and cub, no longer live in Yosemite.

The Grizzly Giant sequoia was named for what was once Yosemite's grandest animal–the grizzly bear. A big grizzly can weigh 800 pounds. But Yosemite's grizzlies are all gone. Most were killed by ranchers, miners, and hunters before Yosemite became a park.

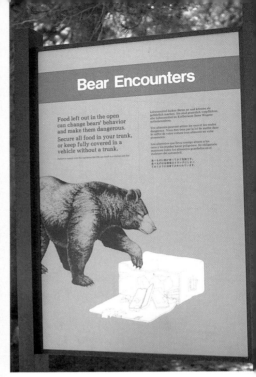

## Bear Encounters

Food left out in the open can change bears' behavior and make them dangerous. Secure all food in your trunk, or keep fully covered in a vehicle without a trunk.

A black bear (left). The sign (above) tells visitors what to do if they meet a bear.

But Yosemite still has hundreds of the grizzly's smaller cousin, the black bear.

Visitors to Yosemite used

to invite hungry black bears into their camps and feed them human food. This was a mistake.

Feeding wild animals makes them forget how to find natural foods. That's why feeding wildlife—big or small—is no longer allowed in national parks. It's best for the animals that way, and safest for you.

All together, Yosemite has five kinds of wildlife: mammals, amphibians, reptiles, fish, and birds.

Bighorn sheep

Mammals are animals
that give birth to live young.
Yosemite has some 77
species of mammals. These
include bears, deer, coyotes,
squirrels, and bighorn sheep.

Ground squirrels (left) and coyotes (right), are some of the mammals found in Yosemite.

There are also some 30 species of reptiles and amphibians in Yosemite. These small animals reproduce by laying eggs. And they hibernate, or sleep, through each winter. Amphibians need to live

The western racer snake and the western whiptail
lizard (inset) are some of the park's reptiles.

near water, but most
reptiles do not.

The most familiar reptiles
are snakes and lizards.
Common amphibians
include frogs and toads.

Eleven species of fish
swim in the lakes and

Rainbow trout (left) and western toad (right)

streams of the park. The
most common are the
rainbow trout. Trout are fun
to catch and tasty to eat.
Park rangers will tell you
some good places to fish.

Birds are the most
common wildlife in Yosemite.

35

More than 240 species of birds live all or part of every year in the park. These include noisy woodpeckers, soaring hawks, and night-hunting owls.

Red-tailed hawk (above) and yellow-bellied sapsucker (right)

Great gray owl mother and chicks in their nest

The best way to see
some of Yosemite's wildlife
is to spend time in the
woods, camping and
hiking.

37

# YOSEMITE'S GREAT OUTDOORS

The park has only 450 miles of roads, but it has 800 miles of foot trails. Many of Yosemite's trails are short. They lead to waterfalls, lakes, and other

A foot trail leads into the forest at Yosemite.

interesting places. Others are long enough to keep you hiking all summer.

For a long hike into the park's backcountry, you must carry a backpack

People of all ages enjoy hiking in Yosemite.

loaded with food and camping equipment. That way, you can camp wherever you are.

But most Yosemite campers stay in roadside campgrounds. Most of the park's eighteen campgrounds are located in pretty places, and they have toilets and running water.

Opposite page: Tioga Lake and Tioga Pass, near the eastern entrance to Yosemite National Park.

# JUNIOR RANGERS

Park rangers lead hikes
and give talks. They know
a lot about nature.
If you are between the

Park employees give talks on tours (below).
Rangers patrol the park (right) to make
sure that visitors have a safe
and enjoyable stay.

ages of 8 and 12, you can become a Yosemite Junior Ranger. To earn an official Junior Ranger patch, you must attend a Junior Ranger program.

In this fun three-hour program, you will learn about nature and the park. You can find out about Junior Rangers at any park visitor center.

People look very small standing next to the giant sequoias.

At Yosemite National Park, there is something for everyone. No matter what your age, you'll have a giant good time in this place of giants!

Opposite page: The Nevada Fall of the Merced River as seen from Washburn Point.

# WORDS YOU SHOULD KNOW

**amphibian** (am • FIH • bee • yun) — an animal that lives both on land and in water

**cliff** (KLIF) — a high, steep rock face that goes down sharply

**climate** (KLY • mit) — the usual kind of weather and temperature that a place has

**diameter** (dye • AM • ih • ter) — the distance on a straight line through the center of a circle

**equipment** (ih • KWIP • mint) — special tools or supplies that people need to perform a certain task

**glacier** (GLAY • sher) — a thick mass of ice that moves slowly across land or down a mountain

**granite** (GRAN • it) — a hard rock, usually gray or pinkish in color

**hibernate** (HY • ber • nait) — to go into a state of deep sleep in which body temperature drops and breathing slows

**mammal** (MAM • il) — one of a group of warm-blooded animals that give birth to live young, have hair, and nurse their young with milk

**minerals** (MIN • er • ilz) — substances such as iron, gold, or coal that are found in the ground

**naturalist** (NATCH • er • il • ist) — a person who studies plants and animals in their natural setting

**preserved** (prih • ZERVED) — kept from decay or from being destroyed

**reproduce** (ree • pro • DOOSE) — to have babies; to give birth to young

**reptile** (REP • tyle) — a cold-blooded animal that has a backbone and very short legs or no legs at all

**sequoia** (sih • KWOI • ya) — a very large kind of tree that grows in California

**species** (SPEE • ceez) — a group of plants or animals that are of the same kind

**timber** (TIM • ber) — trees that are to be cut down and made into wood for people to use

**trout** (TROUT) — a fish found in lakes and streams that is good to eat

**vertical** (VER • ti • kil) — straight up and down

**wilderness** (WIL • der • ness) — a natural area without towns or farms

**wildlife** (WYLD • lyfe) — living things that are found in the wild; animals that are not raised by people

**Yosemite** (yo • SEH • mih • tee) — a national park in California

# INDEX

## About the Author

*David Petersen is a writer, editor, and college teacher. He lived for several years in California and was a frequent explorer of its national parks.*